Published in the United States by Lulu (www.lulu.com)

ISBN: 978-0-578-01396-1

Victory Is Yours!
Teenage Survival Handbook
(For teenagers, *and* their parents

Sid Taylor, CCP

Lulu.com
W.E.T.M.O.P. Streaks Publishing

Victory Is Yours!
Teenage Survival Handbook
(For teenagers, *and* their parents)

"We are not the healers, nor are we the healed. We are merely witnesses to the miracles of life." - Lakeetha Taylor

I would like to thank first and foremost God, His angels, and all of the Earth angels that made this work possible, and so necessary.
To my wife Lakeetha, my son Khaleef, and my daughter Ariel, I love you and you inspire me to search for the greatness within myself and others. Thank you to my wonderful parents for all you do.

Thank you to all of my siblings as you has inspired me in ways that you will probably never know. And to the good people I have had the pleasure of knowing and learning from in life, I love you all. To everyone that purchased or downloaded this book, I would like to say thank you for your support.

This book is dedicated to the memory of Aunt Eloise, Grandma Odessa, Granddaddy L.C., Uncle Claude, Ryan, Tim, Marcus, Eric, Kevin, Uncle Donald, and all others that have impacted my life directly or indirectly.

Chapters

1. My Journey

2. The immovable object VS The irresistible force

3. Generation "why"

4. Don't mix your drinks

5. Thirst Quenchers

6. Glass Houses

7. "Road" Scholar

8. The Apple and the Tree

9. The Victim

10. The Victor

11. Whose World is it?

Introduction

For years it has been my desire to address what I feel are very important issues regarding the youth of today. It seems to me that the best way to impact a situation is to face it head on, so I have elected to do just that by logging my thoughts on what the majority of the people I speak to regard to be a major problem in today's society. I have decided to title this body of work "Victory Is Yours: The Teenage Survival Handbook", because at the present time most teenagers I have had the opportunity to speak with about their current state of affairs often use the word survival to describe their present state. Some of them view themselves as victims of a malicious and unforgiving system. The word survival is also my word of choice when I get a chance to observe some of their daily routines and activities. Now let's examine the word survival. According to the Merriam-Webster's dictionary definition, survival is described as "the act or fact of living longer than another person or thing". Now that definition strikes me as being totally opposite of what it meant to me to be a teenager during my youth. That definition speaks to me as some sort of competition between peers. It almost sounds like a battle to see who will make it at the expense of those who won't. If I had been asked what it meant to be a teenager I doubt seriously that the word survival (or victim for that matter) would have even been a thought. This makes me ponder the condition that we as adults have allowed to come into existence for our children. That's right I said it, and I'll say it many more times throughout these pages, so get used to it. We have allowed this condition to exist. It's easy to point the finger at "the younger generation" as if they just mysteriously appeared on this planet wreaking havoc and creating chaos instead of being the product of an environment, and atmosphere that we chose to raise them in. I remember being told a long time ago by a wise person, that whenever you point the finger at someone, there are three fingers pointing right back at you. The three fingers in this case would represent parents, environment, and education. While we agree that a lot of decisions that our children are making today don't meet with our approval, we must take some sense of ownership for the conditions that we allowed to exist during their most formative years. Once again, while my goal here is not to point fingers I will be pointing out, however, that since everyone on some level has played a part in the creation of this current condition, we must all do our part to help reverse the situation. I have kept this work as short and concise as possible to ensure that it would be an easy read that even the youngest of teens would be able to complete while compiling enough information for parents guardians, and any responsible adults that want to make a difference in their communities. I have also intentionally repeated some ideas in this book, to make sure nothing gets overlooked. My perspective is that of a professional working in the field for now over 11 years, and as a Certified Coach Practitioner. It is my hope that this work inspires, enlightens, and educates all who choose to read it. This book is a self published work. Please forgive any occasional typographical errors.

Chapter 1

My Journey

What a wonderful time it is to be a teenager. Now if you're reading this statement in the 21st century, you may be thinking that this is an unbelievable statement, but it is very true. If you are a teenager reading this you are truly living in what a lot of people, myself included, would view as the best segment of your life. Now why would I make such a bold statement when a lot of older (and some younger) people often cite the many challenges that teenagers face in these times. While I do agree with some of their claims to a *small* extent, I would much rather focus on the positives. During your teenage years you are in what I like to refer to as the blueprinting phase of your life. This is the time when, with the right amount of guidance, you have the ability to effectively map out the road to reaching your goals. Now when I speak about mapping out the road to your goals, I am by no means talking about spending countless hours, days and weeks filling out charts and tables, and meeting with all sorts of counselors and mentors. I am merely talking about basically discovering what it is you are interested in, and figuring out how you can make it beneficial to you. Once you've gotten a general idea about something that you think you'd like to do, you can then start to set goals on how to make it a reality. Goals you say? I'm a teenager. What do I care about goals? I'm trying to have fun and hang out with my friends. I don't have time for goals. Well, allow me to enlighten. I'll first start by citing some fond, and, not so fond memories of my teenage years. Let's go back a *umm* few years. The year was 19-- and I was fresh out of junior high school. Believe me when I say that at this time in my life, setting goals was the furthest thing from my mind. I was more interested in rapping (oh yes we did rap back then) and playing football. I didn't know anything about making beats back then so I would simply buy a single record, listen to the instrumental, and then start writing lyrics to it. I always thought of it as just a fun way to spend my time, but as some of my friends began to listen to my recorded verses and commented on how great I sounded, I started to wonder, what if. What if I became serious at this rap stuff? What if I went into a studio and recorded songs for a living? That would be a dream come true. What if *I* could actually get paid doing this? Then I thought to myself, rappers don't make much money. Most of them always talked about hard times and being broke. What's so great about that? Now I know that question might sound a little odd when nowadays rappers that don't have much money at all seem to always talk about how they're rollin' in Bentleys, poppin' cris (Cristal champagne) and blowin' 20 stacks (stacks =thousands of dollars) at the bar every weekend. Trust me when I say that these statements are almost always fiction. Now first of all you have to realize that back then, rap was rarely on the radio, there weren't many studios around, and like only a handful of rap record labels. Plus the few rappers that were on the radio rarely rapped about making any money. They mainly talked about how bad off they had it and how they wish they had a job.

As you would probably figure, rap to me was nothing more than a hobby. Even though in my eyes it was the best hobby ever created in the history of mankind. Pretty strong words huh? Okay let's move on. A few of my friends shared similar feelings about rap. One friend in particular (Ace) convinced me to form a group with him and we started making tapes. There was one other short term member that I can't remember but not for lack of skills. He was really nice on the mic. At present time I can't remember the name of our group, but one thing I do remember is having the time of my life. As a freshman at Withrow High School in Cincinnati, Ohio, I can vividly remember our lunch time festivities in a place we called "The Corner". This was a small area located directly down the hall from the lunch room. We would take turns performing verses for anyone who'd stop to listen. These would be verses that we either wrote the previous night, or in the class we had right before lunchtime (further discussed in a later chapter about how my G.P.A. dropped). Our music would be either us beating on our chest or this one kid (I can't remember his name)

providing the beat box (drum sounds from your mouth). I
remember the first few times we performed in front of 5-10
people. The next few times, I would venture to say there were
about 20 people, and soon our audience became too large for our
quaint little spot. I also remember this other kid that used to rap
in "The Corner" named Dr. Ice who would later change his name
to JB Smooth. He was regarded as one of the most popular
rappers in the city, and had even appeared on local radio stations.
As I think about it, he was one of the first people I ever saw rap
live. I was so impressed with his flow that I let my friends
convince me that I should battle him and take over "The Corner".
So I went home after school, wrote some of my best raps at the
time, and was prepared to challenge him the next day. Back then
a rap battle was just that. There was no violence associated with a
rap battle. No fighting or disrespect. The next day I approached
him with my challenge, but he wasn't interested in battling, he
just wanted to hear my flow and for me to hear his. Instead of
battling, we ended up surprising the entire audience with a double

feature as we traded rhymes back and forth for the entire lunch period. This was a real treat for anyone that happened to be in the area and the most crowded I'd ever seen the corner. It was so crowded in fact that the principal announced that the corner would be off limits from that point on. He even decided to place two vending machines in the area so there would be no room for gathering. One thing I recall vividly when "The Corner" was still our spot, was that the number of girls that would come around to listen to us increased each day. At first I saw this as a good thing. What 14 year old boy wouldn't, but this would be the very thing that eventually led up to the breakup of my group. You see, my partner considered himself to be somewhat of a ladies' man, and after a while he lost his interest in rapping, and began to use the corner as his own personal place to pickup girls. Ironically once he stopped rapping, he began to lose his "celebrity" status, and soon found it harder and harder to pickup girls. He would ultimately rekindle his desire to rap, but didn't approach it with the same hunger and drive that made him a lunchtime legend.

Although he remained one of my very best friends in High School, I decide to move on. I have to say that after this, "The Corner" wasn't quite the same. Still I didn't allow that to become a reason to quit, because like I stated earlier, in my mind this was the best hobby ever created. Even though, I'd adopted a "take it stride" type of attitude after my group split up, it took me years to get back on track and a few years later I found myself as a member of my second group. I remember it well like it was yesterday. I was now a senior in high school, a starting guard/tackle on the football team, and working part-time at a world famous fast food restaurant to pay for studio time. Yeah you heard me right; I was now a recording artist. My first song ever (which unfortunately, I no longer possess) was entitled "Pass the Jam". My DJ (Tragic) and I recorded our first and only song as a group (The Outsiders), and even though we would never record together again, this was a very valuable experience for me. This was the start of something big for me. I had a great time recording a song with one of my very best friends to this day, and was able to learn a lot about the technical side of music recording. We would still get together to write lyrics, and discuss song concepts, but never went back into the studio as a group again. Another one of my very best friends to this day known as DVH The Key Keeper became my manager, and we later formed a super group by the name of <u>Def</u> Row (before the record label, and spelled differently). I was now 22 years old and working full time to support my recording habit. We'd been told about a really nicely equipped, and reasonably priced recording studio known as Beat Box not far from us and this is when I began to think of music as a career. We recruited none other than JB Smooth, and two others (Cutty B, & Casual K) to complete the group. It seemed like we practically lived in the studio, as we recorded at a feverish pace. We recorded as a unit and also as solo artists. At the time, I had a reputation as a very creative writer that used a lot of humorous metaphors. After recording one of my favorite songs to date (To the Highest Extreme), my good friend JB, requested a meeting with me. He told me how much he really liked the song, but expressed concern about something I was doing. He said that something seemed to be missing. When I asked him what he meant, his response was a little troubling. Since at this point I was doing all of the production for the group, I initially thought he was talking about the beat, so I asked him. Is it the kick drums? No, he hesitantly replied. The snare drums, or hi hats? I asked. Are my vocals loud and clear enough? He just looked at me in a strange way. He said 'man I've known you for a lot of years, and I don't think you're reaching for your full potential. At this time I was puzzled, so I just came out and asked him what he was getting at. He went on to tell me that he thought that I was one of the best rappers he'd ever heard, and knew that I had more than enough talent to make it in music industry, but then caught himself mid-sentence and made a profound statement. He said man I hear you, but I don't hear *you*. Okay, so now I'm thinking that we needed to take a break from recording. In my mind JB was tired and needed a few weeks away from the studio. To my surprise he was just fine and proved it with his next statement. Once again he said man "I've known you for a long time", and went on to say "I've met a lot of your family members, and have seen how you interact with them". He was referring to my young nieces and nephews. He said, "You're always teaching them through your words and actions", and 'now this music finally gives you a broader audience'. "When are you going to take heed to your calling, and teach through your music?" He said, "When are you, DOC-ILL (this was my stage name), going to teach and heal people?" Wow, I was blown away. Teach and entertain at the same time? Of course this concept was not new to me at all, as most of my favorite rappers were already doing just that. In fact they are the ones I credit with helping me remain focused throughout my teenage years. While a lot of my friends were into other less productive things, my favorite pastimes were listening to music and making music. I thought to myself, he's right you know. A few days later while planning a late night trip to the studio, I remember my two oldest nephews asking if they could spend a night over their friend's house. I told them not this time. They were disappointed and began to beg me.

They told me that they really wanted to go. I still told them no. The reason for my decision was that while I was very familiar with most of the children in the neighborhood, I didn't know the parents of the children whose house they wanted to stay over. Shortly after making my decision, I was off to the studio. It was about 10:00pm when we arrived, at the studio, and we had planned to stay for about 6 hours. We got a fair amount of work done, but nothing seemed to be flowing completely, so we decided to stop off at our manager's house to review our work and discuss a new strategy to improve our level of productivity. At around 7:30am we were all extremely tired and my manager began dropping us off one at a time. Both Casual K and I stayed in the housing projects known as English Woods. I stayed with my sister and her children, and Casual K stayed with his girlfriend. DVH decided to drop us off first. The next hour would change my life forever. This was about fourteen years ago so the details are a little sketchy. Though I remember the details only fairly well, I do remember the feeling as if it was this year. First, for the sake of clarity, I should say that there are two ways to get into English Woods. The front way is the route the bus takes, and the back hill is the way we would take most times since we lived in the lower area known as the "New". I told my manager to go up the back hill since it was always quicker. As we attempted to go up the back hill, it was either blocked, or backed up so we decided to go around the other way. As we drove around the other way, I can remember hearing sirens. I didn't think much about them, but was a little curious nevertheless. When we finally arrived at our destination we saw crowds of people walking to a particular destination. There had been a fire; A really bad one. I got out of the car to ask questions about what had happened, and found out that there was a burglary, and that the criminal had attempted to cover his tracks by arson. I'm not sure if he was completely aware but in the apartment he burglarized, there slept five little children who'd all been killed by smoke inhalation. As I walked closer to the scene of the crime, I saw five little bodies, all covered with sheets. The smell was so bad that I couldn't stay long enough to ask any more questions, so with a heavy heart I walked around to my house. When I went in the door there was my family, all awake and crying. This was a sad day for everyone in the neighborhood, but what I later discovered was that this apartment, this very apartment that was set on fire was the apartment that my nephews were begging me to spend a night at. Even though I'd spent the entire night awake at the studio and was extremely tired I don't remember sleeping at all that day. I kept thinking that if I'd allowed my nephews to spend a night in that apartment they would have suffered the same fate as those innocent little children. At this point I had about a million thoughts racing through my mind. I was asking myself how a person could do such a thing. I was wondering what those children must have been thinking at their last moments. I was wondering where the parent was, what my nieces and nephews were thinking, when were they going to catch this terrible person, and so many other questions raced through my mind. Another question I can remember asking myself was what I was going to do about the situation. Then it hit me the last thing that went through my mind was what JB said to me. "When are you, DOC-ILL, going to teach and heal"? At this time my manager DVH returned. He had taken everyone else back home and returned to make sure that we were alright. About an hour later, my family had all went back to sleep, and it was just me, my manager, and Casual K sitting in the living room of my apartment. Casual K just came out and said "Man, we need to do something about this". He went on about how people in our neighborhood were dropping like flies, and how he was sick and tired of hearing bad news. DVH responded by saying "what can we do about something that already happened"? Casual K just shook his head and said man, we can't just let this type of stuff happen and not do anything about it. We all sat there quietly and a few minutes later Casual K left. About an hour later DVH left and I decided to try to get some sleep. I lay down for about thirty minutes and it hit me. A song about this tragedy must be done. I went over to Casual K's house with the idea, and he almost instantly responded with the title,

"The Sun Never Shines in the Ghetto". I said , "that's perfect", went home to call JB, and Cutty B with the idea, and about a week later we were at Beat Box records on Flora Avenue recording our best song. This unfortunately was the highlight of my super group Def Row. I really don't remember exactly how we split up, but I know the way we split up wasn't too ethical and that I regretted that for a long time. You see DVH the Key Keeper wasn't just a manager; he was and still is one of my best friends. Casual K and I just sort of left the group without much explanation. We ran into a manager by the name of Big U, changed our name to "Freedom", recorded a classic EP by the name of "Straight to Ya' Dome", and opened shows for some of the most respected groups in the country. This was another great experience for me as I and everyone around me watched my production skills grow and mature. Shortly afterwards, my group split up and I decided to quit rapping. Unbelievable isn't it. The greatest hobby ever created grew too frustrating for me... for a while at least. At the ripe old age of 24 I decided that I'd had enough. People would approach me almost daily asking about my next move. When your next album is coming out, they'd ask. What's your next project going to be, they'd inquire. This went on for months and my reply would always be, I'm not recording anymore. Now I was content with this decision for quite a while, but one day while I was at a record store I ran into a guy by the name of Chestah T. Chestah T is a cousin of one of my close childhood friends, and was a local community radio DJ, and Hip Hop artist who had supported all my musical endeavors by playing my songs and inviting me on his program as a guest host. We had done a lot of shows together and I had been a featured artist on one of his singles he recorded for a Kwanzaa CD he'd planned to release. As we were in the store that day he asked me why I hadn't released any new material for a while, and also commented on how he hadn't seen me in the studio in so long. I responded in my usual way and he was a little shocked. He said he goes through the same thing every so often when he wants to just give up. He then said something that really stuck with me. He said something like songs come and go and so do phases, but the artist is always the artist. In other words if you are an artist, no matter what you are going through at sometime in your life, you'll always return to your art form. I went on to add that sometimes the art helps you get past difficult times. This was a powerful conversation that had me wondering why I would abandon something that I love so. I thought about this for a long time and decided to just let things happen naturally. My new mantra was "whatever happens is meant to be". A few months after adopting my new outlook, I received an invitation from a very intense young man by the name of Scholar Akbar. The invitation was extended to what he felt were some of the most dynamic emcees in the city. I walked into a room of about 25 individuals all with one goal in mind. We all wanted to be heard. We all felt that the world needed to hear us. We spent about 5 hours together talking about our goals, and sharing our backgrounds with one another. We also listened to Scholar's description of his vision of what he thought would be the ultimate collection of music ever compiled. He said that the name of the collective would be called The Watusi Tribe, a name he decided on mainly because of their warrior spirit and strong sense of family and tradition. As I listened, I began to think to myself, "this is happening for a reason", so I along with everyone else in the room agreed to come together. We immediately agreed to record an album that Scholar titled Millennium Music. We had the time of our lives recording this CD, and took advantage of every opportunity we had to perform as many songs from the album that we could. I vividly remember "The Rooftop Jam". This was an entire performance that we did on the roof of a store downtown on Linn Street. We followed this momentum that we had and recorded our second album entitled The Cleansing. This was widely regarded by most local critics as a masterpiece. We were often referred to as the next big thing in music, but our numbers had dwindled down from 25 members to 8 dedicated musicians. Our third CD featured 5 emcees and 1 DJ. This was probably our best work ever, but midway through the project I began to have the feeling that there was something else that I should be doing, and a few years later, I decided to leave the group. You see at the time of my decision, I was in school studying Audio and Video production and had a little too much on my plate at the time. I was attempting to put my all into music, my all into school, and my all into a very challenging career. My decision was that I'd finish school first while working full time and then possibly return to music, but once I finished school I decided that I needed to focus on improving my performance and effectiveness in my career as the supervisor of a group home for at risk youth. At the time I was seven years into a very rewarding, yet challenging job that consisted of teaching young men to love themselves enough to do what's best for them. Unfortunately a lot of the young men we dealt with were so convinced that the world had nothing to offer people in their situation that they'd be better off just giving up. Anyone working in this field will likely agree with me when I say that one of the most frustrating obstacles or hurdles in this field is trying to convince someone else why they should care about their own life. There is almost a willingness on the part of some of these young men to ruin their own lives as a way of "getting back" at their parents, or the system. I never understood the concept of "hurting me to hurt you". Nevertheless this belief is alive and *well* (for lack of a better word).

Exercise

What was one of the most influential moments in your

life?

What is it you like to do most (hobbies, interests), and how could you turn this into a career?

What are your long term goals?

What are your short term goals, and do they lead you to your long term goals?

Chapter 2

The immovable object
VS
The irresistible force

In my experiences dealing with at risk youth, I'd often ask myself one question over and over, and at this point you might be asking me the same question. I used ask myself, why should I care about a population of individuals who obviously don't care about themselves? Now I know better than to ask that question. I don't mean to imply that I don't care about them anymore. What I mean is that I no longer feel that the question is valid. We all care about ourselves don't we? How else can we explain the fact that when we feel threatened or in danger, our immediate response is to do whatever we need to do to remove ourselves from harm's way. We'll run, cover up, duck, hide, fight, or do whatever we need to do to feel safe. We all care about ourselves, but sometimes we are confused about who we really are, and what's best for our particular situation. I don't think that too many people will disagree with me when I say that we all want to be happy. Now if we all, no matter whom we are, or what our background is desire happiness, then why would we purposely do things to bring us unhappiness? When I ask these young men this question, I rarely get an answer. When dealing with young people, I find it easier to make my point by using very visual examples. One of my favorite examples is the one involving a trip from my hometown of Cincinnati to California. It goes like this. Now if I wanted to go to California from Cincinnati the first thing I need to know is where California is. The next thing I might do is purchase a map. I have to also determine my method of travel. Okay now I have a map, a car and now I'm ready to go. So far so good, right? That's when I throw them a curve ball. I'll say to them, now what if I decide to throw the map out of the window, as soon as I pull off. Their response would immediately be, you'll get lost. Now in this example we have discovered that if I have a destination with no map, it's not very likely that I'll reach it. This is my way of showing them that if you have a goal with no plan, you are going to have a lot of difficulty in reaching it. Another lesson in this example is if you do have a plan to reach your goal, but for whatever reason, choose not to follow it; your goal will be a lot less attainable. The youth of today are much more intelligent than we give them credit for, and extremely creative, so it seems to me that the more creative I become when teaching, the better my results. The old practice of sitting them down to listen to a stern lecture about why their generation doesn't measure up to ours of the "good old days" just doesn't seem effective anymore. To be honest I don't really know if that method was ever effective. I can remember the times as a youth when I was the recipient of these stern lectures. I just sat there waiting for it to be over instead of actually listening to the lesson. Another thing that I focus on is the desire that they seem to have to live up to an image of what has been created by their peers or the media. We are all constantly bombarded by images on TV, radio, and the internet telling us what we should do, who we should be and, why we can't live without the things and philosophies they offer. We've all fallen victim to irrational decisions, and impulse purchases based on what we've been told is hot, or a must have item. I've often made such a purpose only to later think to myself "what in the world was I thinking?" Why should our children be any different? When I was coming up as a youth I can remember a familiar question just about all adults in my life would ask me. I know most if not all of you were asked the same thing. Teachers, pastors, uncles, aunts, neighbors, and any other adult in my life would ask me what I wanted to be when I grew up. I would always tailor my answer to whoever was doing the asking, but never really gave much thought to the question itself. Now when I'm dealing with young men, and women, instead of asking them what they want to be when they grow up, I find it more appropriate to ask them what their interests are. I feel that once you discover what your interests are you have a much easier time figuring out what you really want to be or do. When we focus on what we want to be when we grow up, we often find ourselves in career choices that are money motivated instead of doing what truly makes us happy. All of the money in the world without happiness often leaves the riches people we can imagine feeling uninspired, and with a reliance of searching for pleasure in prescription drugs, alcohol, sex, and whatever items they can purchase to impress, and please others. Great paying jobs are wonderful, but why not strive to have a great paying job doing something you love. For example, in one of the programs I ran I had a young man that seemed to be preoccupied with drawing shoes. He was in the program because he was caught selling drugs. When I asked him this question, he told me that he loved to draw, and also loved to collect shoes. I suggested to him that he put the two together. Why not become a shoe designer? Now I don't know if this particular young man decided to follow my advice, but so many of the young men I deal with have the ability to change their lives but don't know how, or where to begin. Often times I'd sit these guys down and present them with a blanket question directed at whoever wants to answer and we'd all realize that they all have unique talents, but one challenging question in common. Where do I begin? "How do I get started?" they'd all ask. That's when I ask them a follow up question. How do you eat an elephant? You eat it one bite at a time. How do you run a marathon? You run it one step at a time. More importantly how do you live your life? By this point they would usually see my pattern and answer one day at a time. Now these questions might seem a bit trivial, but they are all true in principle. Everything in existence happens one moment at a time. As a child you are constantly growing, and developing, and the same is true for our teenage years. Teenagers are constantly soaking in the influence of the people they hang around, and attempting to figure out how they fit in. As I think back to my teenage years I remember how my development seemed to happen in 2 or three month segments depending on who I was around at a particular time. This was a time in my life when my friends' opinion seemed to matter so much, and shape my decisions. I wanted to dress like my friends, go to their schools, have the same friends they had, and pretty much do just about everything they did. While at Withrow High School in Cincinnati, and as a member of the football team I'd often hang with teammates after the games and during the off season, even though I knew in my heart that we had nothing in common outside of playing football. Why did I do that? I did that for the same reason teenagers hang together, join clubs, groups, and even gangs. Everyone wants to feel accepted. Everyone including adults want to feel as if they are a part of some exclusive group that requires certain skills and talents that not everyone possesses. While dealing with the young men I mentor, I often hear them get into meaningless arguments, and debates about whose neighborhood is the toughest, or whose school has the best looking girls. We see this in all aspects of life for example I've been to sports bars and witnessed grown men argue to the point of fist fights about who's team is the best, or who has the most loyal fans. I've also heard countless stories about people having their tires slashed, or even their windshield busted solely because their car had the logo of an opposing team at a sporting event.

This mentality even spills over into the minds of our most trusted public officials. I've often watched in disgust, the way political commercials attempt to sway the publics' opinion through the use of smear tactics, and campaign on the strength of what could only be described as genuine hate for their opponent. You know the saying, you are what you eat. Well the same thing goes for what you see and hear, and this "younger generation" that I hear people complain about so much are only mirroring what they see and hear. We are their role models. We are their living breathing examples of what to do, and what not to do. So how do we change these things about our children? The answer is so simple yet most people choose not to believe in it. We can change things by being the change we want to see. For example I don't use profanity around my son for a lot of reasons but mainly because I don't want him to use it. How could I tell him that profanity is wrong or offensive if he hears me, the person he looks up to, use it. We as adults in general, seem to live in a world of "do as I say not as I do". How then, do we expect a teenage male or female to understand the value of a man's (or women's) word, and the true meaning of integrity? Wouldn't you agree that our actions are much more powerful than anything that we could tell our children to start or stop doing? Like the saying goes, actions speak louder than words. The reverse sides of this is when children have positive role models right in front of them each and every day, but choose to follow a self-destructive way of living and decision making. In my many, many years working with juvenile offenders and at risk youth, I am astonished at the number of them that were raised in what a lot of people would describe as a "good" family. This is the direct opposite of what society teaches is the key to raising a productive citizen. What then went wrong? In a lot of these situations I noticed that both parents were in the household, and making good salaries. We must not forget the incredible power of peer pressure, and influence of the media. This is not a flimsy excuse or use of television, and other forms of media as a scapegoat. It simply is what it is. I conduct numerous group sessions with these young men and can remember vividly a comment one of the guys made about this lifestyle (criminal activities) being the American dream. I gave pause at first in disbelief, but couldn't control my urge to ask him what I thought to be an obvious question. Is this the American dream? Is your American dream to amass great sums of money and material items, while living in fear of the next man attempting to take it from you at the first opportunity he gets? Is your American dream to somehow find a way to protect this large sum of money from fellow dreamers only to have everything you've struggled to get taken away by way of police drug bust? I view this in my opinion as an American nightmare, when after all of your assets are seized you don't even have any money for a good lawyer. You'll be forced to watch in desperation as your overworked public defender loses your case, and to make matters worse, your mother has to take a second mortgage on her house for bail money. I was watching a program on television about a very prominent drug dealer that at his peak was generating about two million dollars a day (yeah, you heard me right), and was considered untouchable until he was a victim of a drug bust. At his peak, he was said to have some very powerful and influence people on his payroll. After the drug bust, he lost everything. All of the cars, money, houses, and most "friends" were gone. Imagine that. He went from millions a day to virtually penniless. So I ask you again, what it all for was. I love these young guys in my program, and it might sound strange, but I even love the determination of street hustlers. After all these guys will stay up all day and night to achieve their goals. They'll put everything else that they don't see as being important off to reach their established goal. Who wouldn't love that level of commitment? What I don't love is the fact that all of the intellect that it takes to run such an operation is wasted when these guys get caught. Let's look at this great level of intellect they possess for a moment. Intellect is a gift. It is similar to a tool. To make my point a little clearer, let's examine the usefulness of a common everyday tool. Any tool will work but, for this example we'll use a screwdriver. Now we all know how useful a screwdriver can be. It can be used to repair an automobile, tighten the leg on a table, or to fix a child's bike. There is no doubt in my mind that a screwdriver is a wonderful invention. It is without question a great tool to own, but the same tool used in a different way, can be used to break into a car, pry open a locked door to steal something, or even as a weapon to kill. So while I love the tool of intellect, I don't love when it's used to hurt others. I also don't love what this self destructive cycle does to the mind, and will of these young men. I often ask myself, what I can offer these guys that will help them see the light. Unfortunately most of them immediately discount anyone, no matter how dynamic their words are if they don't represent the imagery of what they so desire. One day I was talking to my guys about self respect and determination. I was on a roll, and it felt as if I was making progress with most of them when out of nowhere, one guy interrupted me to inquire about a jacket I was wearing. "How much did it hit you for?" he asked. Then all the progress that I was making was overshadowed by the others who were now curious about my jacket, and how much they would need to get one. I quickly responded by saying "the cost of my jacket is not important", only to have another notice a watch that my wife had given to me for my birthday. One guy then asked me how much you make an hour. My reason for pointing this out is because it seemed that no matter how powerful my words were to them, they couldn't get past the symbols that they thought were measures of success. Why this fascination with material things, and how do we get past the imagery they so aggressively want to obtain? Since I'd experienced this many times before, I chose to twist it around by asking them questions about their value systems. I think we have to show them with our actions that while material possessions are wonderful, they're only the tip of the iceberg. I also think that if most people were given the option of having either all the material items they ever wanted or true blue friends in their life forever, a great deal of them would pick the material items. This would be a no-brainer for most, but I ask you, when most people come into large portions of money, or purchase large expensive items, what's one of the first things they do? They usually call up one, or more of their closest friends, and take great pleasure in sharing the good news with them. My point is that all the money or possessions in the world are nothing without someone to share them with. This is the same for our accumulated knowledge. All the information in the world is nothing without having someone to teach it to. We can't take our worldly possessions with us, so why should we attempt to take our wisdom to the grave. So after I present the young men with similar questions, obviously I get similar answers. It then becomes obvious to me that if we are more patient with the youth, and present things to them in a more cognitive method, we learn that the difference in our thinking is not as great as we are often led to believe. When we embrace this philosophy, this so called "generation gap" is almost eliminated, and we get the added treat of learning from the very ones we teach. We have to remember that as we age, we are not always as informed as we think we are. This is not limited to slang and fashion, but rather a philosophical, and cultural standpoint. As we evolve as a race

(I'm speaking of the human race), our desires evolve. In my years working with these young men and women I am very grateful to them because I have learned as much from them as they have learned from me. The key to teaching as I have discovered over the years is to use the speak, and listen method. This method is very important because it gives everyone involved a since of purpose during dialogue. Quite frankly, not many people want to just sit and listen to anyone talking for long periods of time without having the opportunity to respond. The same goes for the person doing the talking. Most people don't enjoy doing all of the talking without ever receiving feedback. This statement rings true for many, but in our society we as adults have a bad habit of lecturing our children to death without giving them an opportunity to have any input. We often complain about their music, the way they dress, talk, and even the way they walk. We do this without hesitation, but never even consider the fact that they have minds of their own, and are in no way obligated to think the way we do. Even so we expect them to agree with our opinions, and blindly follow our footsteps. We take every opportunity we can to tell them what they are doing wrong by pointing out all of their flaws in thinking, and view any disagreement on their part as a sign of disrespect. I can't imagine talking to anyone for an extended period of time without receiving any feedback. If I'm going to just talk, and talk without ever receiving any feedback, I might as well just stand in front of the mirror and babble on to myself. That brings me to another point. When we talk to our children about their shortcomings do we ever consider looking in the mirror and consider our own issues, and mistakes. Do we even take time to listen to our own advice? And what about the time when we were children and our parents pointed out things to us about our choices? Did we always listen to their points of view? More importantly, would we be the people we are today if we did everything our parents told us to do? I am by no means advising anyone to disobey their parents, or encouraging parents to stop giving their children instructions or advice, but sometimes I think that too much advice can have the opposite effect on children. I also believe that some of the best lessons we can learn in life are the ones that come from making our own mistakes and correcting them by ourselves. And when we do offer advice we'd be wise to make sure that the advice we give is based on actions that we ourselves take. We are their role models aren't we? Don't get me wrong here. We do have a duty to guide, and assist our children during their development, but we also have to realize that they are individuals with their own thoughts, goals, and dreams. How many of us are currently in the same career field as our parents? We don't always grow up to have the same goals, dreams, and tastes as our parents. While it is true that some do chose to join the "family business" or follow the family traditions, this is ultimately our personal choice. So why force our children to do exactly what we do. While I would love to see my son follow some of my childhood patterns, I realize that it is he that must ultimately choose his own path. I played football, rapped, and participated in a myriad of activities while in high school, but he is in no way obligated to do any of these things. I want my son to enjoy his journey of learning in school, and in life. Of course I don't want him to struggle, or suffer, and I'll offer him as much assistance I can, but the bottom line is I know that this is his life. I know that when I truly realize this, and begin to live by this principle, I'll have the treat of teaching, and learning from him at the same time.

Critical Thinking

What time in your life do you look back on and say, what was I thinking?

What is it that your parent(s) or guardian has said to you in your life that, even though you might have resisted at the time was very valuable advice?

What method of teaching do you feel you will use with your children. Why?

Chapter 3
Generation "why?"

One thing that I must say about our current generation of youth is that they have to be some of the most inquisitive people that I have ever encountered.   This is a generation that wants to know the reason for everything and if you can't provide them with the answers that they are looking for they will certainly find them. Dealing with the questions of the youth of today can be frustrating, but we must look at the strength of this characteristic. If you were a business owner that depended on a research team to gather critical information for your company who would you want working for you? Would you want someone that accepts any answer from anyone, or would you want the "go getter" on your team that will consider anyone's input, but then seek to back it up with facts? I can remember when my now nine year old son first began mastering the basics of the English language one of his first words was the most powerful. I'd talk to him about everything from the simplest things like using good manners at the dinner, table to more complex matters such as racism, human rights, or the value of friendship, and would always encounter his powerful three letter response. He'd look me square in the eye, pause for a moment, and then ask me why. That one word often leaves the most scholarly well schooled of us at a loss for words. It's a question that can be asked over and over no matter what the reply is, and the teenage mind is full of whys. They are at an age where they're searching for their purpose, and should be free within reason to do what they must to find their calling. This can be a very frustrating time in their lives as the questions they most often ask are those that often seem to involve feelings of limitations. I can remember myself at that age wondering why I wasn't hired for a certain job, or why it seemed to me that isolated groups of people based on race, wealth, or class seemed to have things handed to them while others put in twice as much work with much fewer results. I can empathize with these feelings and burning questions because at this time in our lives we can experience a feeling of overwhelming stress and pressure. Should I go to college, join the military, or get a trade? Teenagers at this time need as much support from their parents and mentors as they can get even though they might not ask for it. The last thing they need is added pressure from their parents. I, myself, subscribe to the philosophy that we serve our children better when we lead by example. We also have to learn to admit that we are not perfect sometimes by allowing our children to see us in our natural states. What I mean by this is that we can't always put on an image of invulnerability. We as adults seem to have this feeling that if teenagers see us in a state on imperfection that they won't respect our lessons. It seems to me to be just the opposite. Have you ever attempted to land a job with one of those companies that do these group interviews? During the procedure they ask a volume of questions that seem to imply that if the person being interviewed doesn't measure up perfectly that they will not be given a chance to show them what he or she is really capable of contributing to their company. They often sit across from the person being interviewed holding clipboards while hanging onto every word. Intimidating isn't it. While this might not be the best example, our children face a similar level of intimidation when we choose to talk to them from a standpoint of perfection. Our kids need to know that not only is it okay to make mistakes, but also that their parents have also had to learn how to do things right by learning how not to do them wrong. I recall a story told by Dr. Wayne Dyer as he vividly recalled a remark made by Thomas Edison after he was asked about his failures he encountered while attempting to create the light bulb. To paraphrase, it went something like this. A person asked him how it felt to fail so many times during his inventing process. He was said to have failed over 10,000 times at his famed invention. Fail, he said. I didn't fail. I just learned 10,000 ways how not to make a light bulb. I make this point to say that our children as well as us as parents must learn the value of what a lot of people would label as mistakes. Remember our children are in many ways just like us, and should be entitled to some of the same learning experiences that we had.   It is said that many inventors would have never given up if they'd realized how close they were to succeeding. I recall being at training for a home-based business I embarked on not too long ago when I heard some very profound words by one of the speakers. Scott Tomer one of the founders, stood up on stage in front of all of us and spoke very eloquently for about an hour, and before he left us he looked into the crowd and said 'if you don't remember anything I said here tonight, remember this.' "It is always too early to quit". When we think of it quitting should not even be an option. Did you know that the great Michael Jordan was cut by his high school basketball coach in the tenth grade? He was actually told that he was not good enough. Now what if he decided to quit? The world would have missed out on sheer athletic genius. Just imagine how many potential superstars like Michael Jordan have quit because someone told them they were not good enough. What about Bill Gates? He "quit" college didn't he? No he didn't quit, he simply re-evaluated his current situation and decided that there was something better for him. He had the courage to ask himself why, in regards to where he was in his life and made adjustments. There are so many others that were forced or had the courage to ask themselves why with amazing results. There were also countless others that simply walked away from something they truly loved based on receiving an undesirable commentary. Remember the immortal words of Mr. Tomer. It is always too early to quit. If you don't want to take his advice, then maybe Beyonce Knowles' advise to simply "upgrade you" might sound more convincing. I think that's just another way of saying reinvent yourself. If you like what you're doing but not necessarily the results then sometimes you might only need to change your approach. I'm not saying that if you're selling drugs and get caught that you should change your method of selling drugs. What I am saying is that if you're trying to get money illegally you might want to think of a legal way to get paid. Why focus all of your efforts on getting paid illegally, staying up at all hours of the night, busting your butt to make a living in a job that allows someone or group (The Judge, or Police) to come along and take it all away. On top of that now you have a criminal record and when you get released from jail you can't get a decent job. So now you figure that you have to do what to earn a decent living? Sell drugs. It's a vicious cycle isn't it? Because every time you get caught you get deeper into the system as you keep getting out and going back, well that is until they decide to give you those football numbers (large number of years in the penitentiary). This is something that plagues our inner city youth because they are often just emulating what they see around them. We as a whole have to get to a place where we see beyond instant gratification and look for a more stable way of existence, as the instant gratification often leads to an instant consequence which also leads to instant subtraction of your hard earned money. I know a lot of people that have amassed an enormous amount of illegal money in their lifetimes (I'm talking hundreds of thousands and in one case millions) only to lose everything they worked for.

Some of these people are homeless now, and one of them has asked me for money recently. So I'll end this chapter in the way that I started it by saying, "Generation... why?"

Critical Thinking

What are some of the challenges that you have experienced as you are working on your goals?

Can you think of anyone you know that possesses unique talents but seem to sabotage their own future? Explain.

After reading chapter 3, what advice would you offer them?

Chapter 4

Don't mix your drinks

It's not the germs that make you sick, or the medicine that makes you well. What heals you or ills you reside within your thoughts.   *- Lakeetha Taylor*

Now you might be scratching your head at this point and wondering why I would choose such a name for a chapter in a book that I have dedicated to helping young people survive. Rest assured, this has nothing to do with alcohol. This chapter, my friends, has a lot more to do with mixing contrasting energies. When dealing with the young men I teach we often have this conversation, and I make it a point to present them with the scenario about the foolish gardener. It seems that there was this gardener that wanted to sell carrots after his next harvest. He said to himself, "there is going to be a great demand for carrots next year so in order to profit from this demand, I must plant twice as many carrots as I usually plant." He immediately went to his shed where he kept his seeds to get ready for planting. To his

surprise there were no carrot seeds left, but instead of going out in

pursuit of more carrot seeds he reached into another drawer and

pulled out tomato seeds. "This will do", he gleefully shouted. So

to his garden he ran and started to plant tomato seeds

everywhere. He thought to himself, about how much money he

stood to make after his next harvest. He phoned as many people

that he could to let them know that he would be ready for their

carrot demands. "Don't forget me when you're ready for carrots

next year" he would say at the end of every conversation. Well

time passed and he was excited. As harvest time grew near,

people would place orders for carrots, and the farmer was very

pleased with what he thought would be his best year yet. When

the next season came around his customers were very

disappointed to find that he didn't have one single carrot. "You

promised us carrots". "What happened?" He replied, "I must

have planted hundreds of tomato seeds". "I don't know what

happened," he said. "I'll tell you what happened," one of the angry customers shouted. "You've gone mad." "How do you possibly expect to get carrots from tomato seeds?" My point of saying don't mix your drinks is just that. If you want carrots, then plant carrot seeds. If you want to get positive results in your life you have to make positive decisions. How could you possibly get positive results from negative actions? How could you possibly desire to live a life of positive, while hanging with a crowd that has the opposite goal in mind? Now here's the million dollar question? Who do people like Donald Trump, Russell Simmons, Bill Cosby, Warren Buffet, Oprah, Magic Johnson, and Bill Gates, and so many more of their peers hang with? They hang with money makers, because they are money makers. Well I guess in the case of most of those people, you could call that the billion dollar question. Who do gang members and white supremacist hang with? In other words like energy attracts. So if you want to be rich, it would probably benefit you to hang with likeminded individuals that are either rich or on their way to achieving wealth. This advice is not exclusively directed to teenagers.

Parents that seek to raise their children in productive ways might want to steer clear of parents that don't have the same wish for their children. Who do you think your children will hang with? This explains why a lot of wealthy parents decide to send their children off to boarding schools to mingle with children of other wealthy families who have made the same decision. Now I'm definitely not saying that I support any sort of class or race theories such as the belief that one group of people are superior to any other group. I without a doubt don't believe in the ideology of groups or clubs that operate on the principle of complete exclusion of certain groups. What I am saying is that the more positive influences you place in your life the greater the likelihood that your results will be desirable. Now this philosophy works both ways. What I am really saying is the more negative elements that you allow to exist around your children, the higher the likelihood of producing negative results. I have dealt with some young men whose parents are viewed as being cool simply because they smoke weed with their children, and provide alcohol and cigarettes for them and their friends. These are some of the same parents that are often heard making comments about their children such as "I don't know where he went wrong or he wasn't raised to live like this." We live in an age of information and I don't feel that anyone should ever be deprived of at least an opportunity to prove their worth. That being said, we as parents and role models (yes I said it, we are role models whether we want to be or not) need to realize that we play a major part in the productivity or lack thereof of the younger generation. I call everyone role models simply because no matter what color you are, or what your age is somewhere someone is watching you. Someone is being influenced by your actions whether you want them to or not. This works in many ways. While committing negative actions some are attracted to your behavior, and some are motivated to never turn out like you did. While living a positive lifestyle, some are extremely impressed, and some are repulsed, calling you a sellout or a lame. They might vow to follow in your positive footsteps, or might feel moved to be the anti-you.

I'd be remised if I didn't take this opportunity to speak about the importance of giving ethical guidance to our children. I've dealt with countless young men that come into the program with very narrowly, warped points of view that obviously had to have been coached to them by people who don't posses anything close to a universal way of thinking. What I mean by this is when children grow up around people that have less than flattering opinions about anyone that exists outside of their ethnic, cultural, racial, or economic surroundings, and they openly express this to these children, there is a good chance that these children will grow up viewing the world through these same stereotypical binoculars. What does this say about our current state of affairs? The very things that we dispose and complain about began with either our own behaviors, or with behaviors and beliefs that we collectively failed to challenge when we had a chance to do so. Our children are mirror images of the adults that they grew up observing, and if they grew up in a household that thrived on a steady diet of hatred, bigotry, less than flattering views toward the opposite sex, or any other low vibrating thoughts then that's what they will view as normal and acceptable. By this time I'm sure that just about everyone has heard about the law of attraction. Like two of my favorite authors Esther and Jerry Hicks say "you get what you think about, whether you want it or not". Hatred only produces more hate. Needless to say, we are *all* role models whether we want to be or not. That being said, I think it's worth adding that we need to be as positive a role model as possible.

Critical Thinking

When you look at your current situation, and think about your goals, do they match up? Explain

What type of peers do you have in your life, and do they bring you closer or further away from your goals?

Do you feel that your actions match your ambitions in your life?

Chapter 5

Thirst quenchers

"Some say your attitude determines ya' latitude" -
Kanye West

As I mentioned earlier I the introduction of this work, it is
important to me to be engaged in the solution to anything that I
view as a problem. Now having said that what I have to realize as
well as you, the reader, is that you can't solve any problem with
the same energy that created it. I often encounter those who talk
about how much they hate violence, racism, discrimination, and
many other hate based issues, while vibrating on the same energy
level. We march at rallies against this and that, but often offer the
same level of hate and anger as the thing that we so dislike. This
is what I refer to as the kill or be killed mentality. Example: "I
hate all those thugs that are out there killing people; they should

be put to death". I've heard countless young men justify carrying guns, by telling me how they only do so to protect themselves. I ask them why they would carry guns, and what they would do with the gun when confronted by their "enemy". "I'd kill him, most would reply". "I'll get them before they get me". So if I understand you correctly, you'd kill them, and then go to jail for life. Simple math tells us that two lives would be cut short. One dead and one removed from society. My point is that you cannot possibly solve a problem with the same energy that it originated from. Another great example of this would be of someone who has a drinking problem, or a perhaps a drug addiction. If you have become an alcoholic, or a drug addict, it certainly wouldn't make any sense to think that the solution to overcoming your addiction would be to head to the local bar, or to go spend some quality time with the neighborhood drug dealer. That just doesn't make much sense does it? Neither does it make much sense to complain, as some of the guys I council do about how the police are so thirsty (having a strong desire to lock them up for any reason), while behaving in such ways that give them the opportunity that they claim they seek. This is a hot topic in the group home I work at. "The boys (police) are so thirsty", they often say. My response is usually something like this. Well if you feel that they are so thirsty, then why would you walk around waving a tall glass of water at them? In other words, why would you possibly feel moved to give anyone an opportunity, or better yet, encouragement to do something to you that you say you don't want to happen? Parents, the same goes for you. Why would you drink with your children, or allow them to use drugs in your presence when you don't want them to develop negative habits? I've heard such attempts at justifying these actions by parents who often say, "well if my child is going to drink or do drugs I'd rather have them do it in my presence". Wow! It's bad enough that a child would chose such self-destructive activities, but I can't possibly fathom how it makes it better if any parent were to sit there and watch it. Could you imagine yourself getting a call from a close friend that has chosen suicide as their ultimate fate, and responding to them, "well, I certainly don't agree with that course of action, but if you're still going to go through with it, then I *insist* that you do it in front of me." Now at this point you might be saying, "wait just a minute Sid". How can you possibly compare something like watching someone commit suicide to someone watching a child drink and do drugs? The answer is simple. When you sit down and watch your children behave in detrimental ways such as drinking and doing drugs, you are encouraging them to become apathetic. A lot of the apathetic children that I deal with in some ways are like the walking dead. Some can be resurrected, and some just can't. Now as powerfully disgusting as a response like "kill yourself in front of me" would be, remember, we're not talking about a close friend here, we are talking about your child. This is your own flesh and blood that you're willing to watch go into self destruction mode. Sometimes we as parents do these things for the sake of being "cool". These are the things about ourselves that we have to examine, if we want to create the positive parental environment that we desire. We do want to create a world free of stress, and anxiety don't we? If so then we have to realize that since our world is a reflection of our every thought, and decision, and since every influence we allow our children to have will in turn influence their every decision and thought, then we as parents have to be willing to teach our children as well as listen to them. When we listen to our children, they'll tell us exactly what's on their mind. Their actions, language, friends, clothes, music, and interaction with us will tell us all we need to know about their lifestyle choices, and all we have to do is pay a little closer attention. Rather simple isn't it. Well on paper it always is, but in reality, though it's far from impossible, it does take work. Raising responsible productive children takes time and a lot of patience. Not only do we have to safeguard or children from negative influences, we have to shield ourselves from falling into limited ways of thinking. This includes, but is not limited to passing group judgments. We as parents have to stop being intimidated by our own children. The younger generation, is this, or those project kids are that. As I mentioned earlier, I don't condone nor do I endorse any belief

that deals in the total exclusion of any ethnic, racial, age,

economic, or cultural group of people in its entirety, so I feel very

strongly that we should all be treated and viewed as equal

partners in this life experience. We have to get to know our

children and the friends they spend time with. If we are going to

close this "generation gap" we must not view our children, or any

others for that matter as being separate from ourselves. This is a

very common mistake we make when trying to figure out what

went wrong with our youth. I must admit that at a point in my life

it was a common practice of mine to lay all the blame for my

conditions on one, or a few groups of people. In time I began to

realize that there was only one person to blame for all my

perceived setbacks. There is only one culprit to point out for my

condition. There is only one person deserving of any credit for my

success. This person, as you may have guessed by now is me. We

make the world we live in. Now we do have to acknowledge that

there are many people that come into our lives and play crucial roles in our development, but we also have to realize that we are the writers of our life script. So just as it would be on the set of a movie, seeking consultation for the sake of authenticity is a welcomed practice by most directors, but allowing another to come in and dictate the flow of your film would be unheard of. The same way that it should be unheard of to let someone come into your life, and make all your decisions for you. Imagine if someone were allowed to tell you what to wear, what to watch, who to talk to, what foods to eat, or what jokes to laugh at. That doesn't sound like an enjoyable existence to me. We are all here to enjoy our own experiences and to learn, and teach our own lessons, so to allow someone else to program you like some sort of robot or computer program, might not be a great feeling. Now to this, parents must also take heed. How many times have people attempted to tell you how to raise your children? Better yet, how many times have you attempted to tell someone else how they should raise their children? How many times have we, as parents, gone completely overboard when giving our children guidance?

This is a very fine line to walk because, this method, if we're not careful, can lead to us trying to completely run (or better yet ruin) or children's lives instead of offering the support they so greatly desire, and need. When we adopt this method of making our children's decisions for them what usually happens? Remember the old saying "in one ear and right out the other". No one wants to be constantly told what to do. We have to learn to balance the art of giving and receiving. The yin and yang principle rings through loud and clear when raising our children. While we definitely want to guide them to help them achieve their goals in life, we must resist the temptation to tell them what their goals should be. In this way if we are not careful, we become thirsty to run their lives. My Dad was somewhat famous in Cincinnati as a young man because he was a boxer (and a darn good one) and sparred numerous times and grew up with one of the most famous, if not the most famous boxer of them all. When I tell you that my dad grew up in Louisville, Kentucky you'll probably deduce that the famous boxer that I'm speaking of is none other than Muhammad Ali. Boxing was in his blood and my two oldest brothers shared his passion for pugilism. I, on the other hand didn't feel the same way. While I really liked boxing, and do to this day, I just couldn't muster up a good enough reason to stand in front of someone and trade blows. Football was more my speed, and as I mentioned earlier rapping was and is my passion. My dad really wanted his sons to enjoy the things that he enjoyed, but knew not to force us into doing exactly as he did. Our choices regarding our hobbies and goals were completely up to us. With that being said, I want you to know that I want you, the reader, to enjoy every facet of your life, but ultimately it is up to you.

Critical Thinking

Have you ever hung out with out with a group of people that you knew
you had nothing in common with?

What do you think makes people behave in such manners?

Chapter 6

Glass houses

"Someone's opinion of you doesn't have to be your reality." - Les Brown

Have you ever heard the cliché "people in glass houses shouldn't throw stones?" I used to hear this all the time. It would usually be someone's response after they heard another person gossiping or complaining about someone, and as a child I would always wonder what it really meant. This is a clever way of saying that we should be very mindful of the stereotypes, and judgments that we make on a daily basis regarding our views of how others around us should look, act, and think, smell, talk, etc. . Now if this sounds a little redundant after I've already touched on this a bit, I'll qualify my repetition by stating the importance of our being as objective as possible when viewing others' behaviors. This is a topic that I cannot stress enough and one that if you take heed to, can instantly change the world as you know it. We must learn to stay focused on our own lives, and purposes instead of being consumed by the lives and activities of others. I can remember conversations that I have had with many close friends, and relatives that started off harmless enough and ended up in heated debates. These conversations were often the result of a comment that someone made about a specific group of people. Why do we find it so important for others to fit in roles that we have created for them? Any time a friend or family member behaves in a way that we are not completely used to we see this as odd, and insist that they change their ways immediately. One of my friends once told me one day that I should really think about not associating too much with white people. I was stunned when I heard this. I immediately asked him why he would make such a statement, and he couldn't give me much of a response. The only thing he really said was that they didn't like us and we shouldn't bend over backwards to please them. "They", I said. Do you mean to tell me that you feel that every person in this group of people feels the same exact way as everyone else in their particular demographic? He said not really, but you know how "they" are. There was one of those four letter words that I really don't want to familiarize myself with. Excuse me, Mr. Perot (for "you people" that are old enough to remember). A little advise to all readers. Anytime someone you know or not begins to speak about certain groups of people, and uses the words them or they, or places them in a commonly specific category, I'd advise you to be really careful in involving yourself in the conversation. I myself don't like being involved in any conversations involving what "they" did or how we shouldn't trust or like "them". These are words that usually indicate, or at times encourage separation from others and this sort of belief system, in my opinion leads us away from our true purpose. If we are going to advance as a civilization, or if our children are going to advance as a generation, we must look to our union as human beings as opposed to our separation as races or ethnic group. I can remember watching movies that dealt with the struggles of African-Americans, and in the movies they'd be showing a protest scene where people would yell out vulgarities at the marchers. In these scenes there would always be disturbing images of small Caucasian children yelling out obscenities at the marchers alongside their parents, and I would be reminded that hate and the desire for separation are learned behaviors. When a child is born there is no hate, despair, feeling of superiority, inferiority, guilt, or any other low vibrating emotions. We create that world for them. We show them with our words and actions that this is the way the world works. Here's an example of what I'm speaking of. Traditionally in most hospitals whenever a child would be born, what was the first thing that the doctor would do? They would smack the child. Why would this be done? It has been said that this act was necessary to clear the mucus out of the lungs, thus allowing the baby to take his/her first breath. Well to this day I'm not entirely sure about that, but what I do know is that they are introducing these precious and innocent beings to fear and pain. Just imagine being awakened every morning out of a peaceful sleep with a swift and stern smack to the face. What do you think your day would be like if you were forced to start it out that way? This is what I call starting your day of by getting up on the 'wrong side of the bed'. This is no different than a lot of parents' practices of introducing their young children to hate, greed, materialism, separation, feelings of superiority, or inferiority lack, unworthiness, shame, etc.... . We do this in many ways. We do this when we set the negative examples like the one that I mentioned earlier, or worse, when we sit idly by as others behave in such ways. This is like saying, "son/daughter, although we don't display these horrid behaviors, it would be rue or disrespectful if we spoke out against others who do". Contrary to popular belief, not standing up for all human rights is just as bad. What makes these practices so bad is the fact that a lot of parents are not even aware of this. We often feel like negativity is not a bad thing for our children to be exposed to as long as we're not directly responsible for it. Have you ever been around people that racist jokes? When they make these jokes, even if we are not the ones laughing, our silence sends a message of approval to them.

Critical Thinking

Think of a time in your life when you may have heard someone make a joke about someone and you laughed.

Instead of laughing is there another way you could have handled the situation?

Chapter 7

"Road" Scholar

As I have been indicating throughout most of this work, it is extremely important to not only have a blueprint for success, but to follow it closely. Let's examine another one of my (hundreds of) examples that I use when dealing with the young men I counsel. Let's say that we have plans to travel to Kansas City, and we put *you* in charge of transportation. You're equipped with a very detailed road map telling you exactly how to get from Cincinnati to Kansas City. You start off on your way, and by some unfortunate "turn" of events, you take the wrong exit. Instead of turning around, you decide to keep going the wrong way. Now in today's age of technology, let's imagine that you also have one of those fancy GPS systems, and it tells you that you passed your exit, but you choose to keep going. At this point you begin to feel lost and decide to stop at a gas station for directions. Now let's not forget that you already have a GPS monitor that's telling you that you are going the wrong way, but for some reason you don't trust it and want to get directions from a real live person. When you tell the person what your destination is, he looks at you strangely and responds by stating "mister, your way off course". He attempts to give you an alternate route that will take you back to the exit that the GPS has been telling you that you missed, but out of frustration you just walk out of the store and get back in your car. I guess you didn't like the tone of his voice, so you take off, again in the wrong direction. Now by this time some of your fellow passengers are noticing that you are going the wrong way, and start to express their concerns, that you need to turn around. Instead of listening to them, you keep going in the same wrong direction that you had been driving in for some time now. Let's also imagine that you are equipped with a cell phone, and get a call from your mother. She's just calling to see how things are going and when you tell her everything is fine, her response is "great, so how far along are you?" You proudly respond by giving her your location, but are a little taken back by her response. What do you mean I'm going the wrong way? Why are you so worried about what I'm doing? I know exactly what I'm doing, and I know where I'm going. Now by this time, you're beginning to get a little upset, and start to wonder why everyone is suddenly in your business. You can't believe that they even have the nerve to try to tell you what you're supposed to be doing. So you continue on your journey to Kansas City refusing to acknowledge the "whining, and complaining" of anyone around you, and hours later you find yourself in Little Rock, Arkansas. From what I have heard Little Rock is a wonderful place to visit, and to live in, but to your dismay this is not at all where you wanted to be. By now you're beyond furious. You feel a sense of disappointment and even a little guilt for allowing yourself to get to this place, and also for bringing your friends here. After all, they were counting on you to get them to Kansas City. You were in charge of the directions, so to a great degree, you were their leader, and you blew it. How could you have let this happen? How could you have ignored their input when they were only trying to help? What are you going to do now? Now I ask you. How much different is this example from some of the back and forth struggles of youth that don't want to listen to people when they get their priorities mixed up? For example, most of (if not all of) the children in my facility have had people all around them throughout their life letting them know when they had taken wrong turns in their lives, and have chosen to ignore these warnings. When they get to my program I often tell them that they are reaching the point of no return. Now let's go back for a minute to my trip to Kansas City example, and imagine that the travelers only had a specific amount of time, and gas money for their trip with a one fill up and a 2 hour surplus. This would mean that even though it wouldn't be desirable, they could take some wrong turns and still make it to their destination as long as they got back on the right track before they used up too much gas or took too long to reroute. This is the same way our adolescent lives work, as gas would be considered energy (of ourselves or others), and time would be, well... time. These are commodities that can't afford to be wasted, yet most of us waste them like they are in infinite supply. How many times have your teachers, friends, parents, grandparents, godparents', uncles, aunts, neighbors, pastors, counselors, caseworkers, bosses, police officers, P.O.'s, magistrates, judges, staff members at group homes, foster care workers, etc... told you that the road that you were going down would lead to a dead end, only to have you ignore their words? How many chances have you had to make a U-turn and get back on track? Unfortunately, not enough young men and women heed these warnings, and end up in adult facilities, strung out on substances, or in worse case scenarios... the graveyard. Now to reverse this, how many of us parents or other adults are like some of the passengers in the earlier example that sit and wait while the driver is going the wrong way, and only speak when they've gone the wrong way for a period of time that we view as too long. Some only speak up when they feel that the actions of others are beginning to inconvenience them. The time to speak up is when the first wrong turn is taken. Especially when you are a passenger in someone else's car, and are at the mercy of the decisions they make to go the wrong way. Countless time I've dealt with children that have gotten into some type of trouble solely based on the "riding with a driver that was going the wrong way". Often times they sit idly by while someone does something that they know are wrong. We all have to realize that we are not here alone and that the choices we make or don't make, don't only affect us. Every decision we make can have a lasting effect on everyone in our lives, whether we know them or not. If I live in an apartment building and choose to play loud music at 3 in the morning, my actions don't only affect me. Just because I'm not sleepy doesn't mean that everyone else in my building wants to be up all night. I could be preventing the surgeon next door from getting enough sleep, and when he operates on his next patient, he might not be as alert as he needs to be. This not only has an effect on the doctor and his patient, but can have an effect on the patient's family if something goes wrong during surgery. The doctor might then be sued, which might cause him to be unable to send his children to college, which could have an effect on their adult lives. This in turn might prevent them from being able to get a good job, and raise their children in the neighborhood that they desire, and so on. All because I didn't' take into consideration how my life and choices are not only going to affect me. This is all because I wanted to play my music loud at 3 in the morning. Another example would be if I have a pet and allow my pet to use the bathroom all over the curb, a neighbor's child or visitor might step in it and track it into their apartment. Now this person has to hire someone to come in and vacuum and steam clean their apartment. Now what if the person doing the steam cleaning is rather clumsy and accidentally bumps into their mantle over the fireplace that has a vase containing the ashes of one of their beloved relatives. That would be truly disastrous. Now let's remember that this clumsy individual would have never even been in their apartment if I would have picked up behind my pet. Let's take it even further by stating that this clumsy individual wanted to be a lawyer as a child but his dad couldn't afford to send him to the best schools, because he's the doctor in the earlier example that I caused to lose his license when I chose to play my music a 3 in the morning. This is my actions affecting someone else. It gets very deep when you think about it. The thing I would say to parents that choose to drink or do drugs with their children, is don't be surprised when those actions come back to bite you in the butt years down the road. While working in juvenile facilities, I have met a lot of parents that come to me with stories about how "he knows better" or "she was never raised to be this way", or the one where the parent tells me that "my child shouldn't be here", and it always baffles me when I sit and talk to some of them in great length. Some parents really don't make the connection between their actions, and their children's situation. It really doesn't dawn on some of them that their child is either a product of the environment that they created for them, or the result of their negligence to intervene. Our every choice that we make as parents, especially during our children's' earliest years, provides a living example or blueprint of what the world is all about. Our children in turn grow up and act according to what they view the world to be, and this is what they begin to teach their children, and so on. Now I am not at all implying that all of the parents of the children that I deal with are the cause of their situations, but I think that it needs to be said that we all have a very profound impact on our children's lives and can truly make a difference when we identify this connection. The question then is, how do we make that connection, and after it's made what we can do to make a positive change occur. Those two questions will be addressed in the final chapter.

Critical Thinking

Can you remember a time in your life when you were making a poor choice in your life and someone was there to give you some good advice?

Did you follow their advice?

If you didn't follow their advice, do you wish you did?

Chapter 8

The apple and the tree

Now we have all heard the saying that the apple doesn't fall too far from the tree haven't we? But what does it really mean? Of course we understand that it is saying that our children will not be too much different than we are, but I would like to go a little deeper than the cliché meaning. I'm speaking on a level of how everything that we allow ourselves to come in contact with throughout our entire life including, but not limited to the programs we watch on television, the radio stations we listen to, the companies we work for, the neighborhoods we chose to live in and so much more. I honestly feel as though we make our choices in life based on magnetic attraction. Like I say to the young men I counsel when they have gotten themselves into an undesirable situation, it is partly your fault. What is it within you that allowed you to get into that situation? What energy have you allowed to come into your world that supports your current reality? The apple in my view is the person and the tree is everything that they willingly or unwillingly allow to become a part of their lives. The tree would consist of role models, friends, media, parents etc. I can remember listening to a recent internet radio program on Hay House Radio hosted by Dr. Wayne Dyer in which he made a very strong point about how our children are choosing role models based on popularity instead of character. I listened as he spoke about two young celebrities that are struggling with addiction, and how this, to some children is viewed as some sort of cool "rite of passage". I also experience this way of thinking directly while working at the group home. Some of the guys actually challenge my credibility when I tell them that I've never been to jail. I respond to them by stating, I think a person that has been in similar situations as you guys are in could serve as a very powerful teacher, but let's face it. Who would you rather learn about finances from, Bill Gates, or the guy that might earn a lot of money fast, but always find a way to lose everything? I don't think that anyone that wants to be a millionaire has included in their list of goals that they would like to lose their money along their road to wealth. We have to realize that the very ones we choose to be are role models are indeed, a reflection of us. When I look at some of the images that I see on TV and in the media in general, I am appalled. Our children are encouraged to follow the images of very low vibrating celebrities that seem to be forced into portraying themselves in ways that they probably wouldn't choose if they had a choice. In my lifetime, I have had the pleasure of meeting some entertainers, and have been pleasantly surprised that they are nothing like the image they portray in the media. On occasions that I have had to question them, most reply by stating that their manager or other handlers have created this persona in order to sell records, or movie tickets. On the other hand, I have seen some of the celebrities that the young men in my counsel look up to, and only come to one very harsh and disappointing conclusion. This might sound judgmental on my part, and even out of line to some, but on *some* levels, and in *some* cases, our children are actually admiring (for lack of a better description) future dope fiends, and prostitutes. I often challenge my guys to visualize these guys, and young women that they look up to 10 years down the road. A lot of these celebrities are dealing with serious addictions, which, if it weren't for their careers, would land them in very different environments. I was listening to a radio station one day and was really shocked as the guys were actually rooting for these artists as they bragged about how much ecstasy, syrup, or lean (a mixture of cough syrup and alcohol), sherm (PCP), cocaine, laced joints (marijuana mixed with cocaine, or dipped in one of many chemical solutions), liquor, vicodin, oxycontin, and so many other substances that they frequently consume before I eventually blocked out before changing the station in disgust. Would you believe that they actually got upset with me? I was watching the news a few days ago and they were doing a story about several young female celebrities that had been recently caught on tape intoxicated, gotten arrested, been sued for going into sudden fits of rage for no reason, and two stories about

2 artist that had taken public falls apparently as a result of being too drunk to perform. The surprising part about this is that the story was portrayed in an almost joking manner. It seems to me that we are actually promoting the very activities that we say we want to end. So in my earlier example, we are the tree, and our children are the apples. It is really ironic that athletes get suspended, and kicked out of their respective leagues for violating substance abuse policies, while their bosses make a huge income from beer sales, at the games, and commercials during their televised events. What message are we really sending when we profit off of the same thing we punish people for. Where is our responsibility, and accountability? We have waged a war on drugs, but every five to ten minutes, I see a commercial telling us that we need to consume more pills. In one conversation we are telling children that trying to escape from their problems with drugs and alcohol is wrong, but it's okay when we constantly tell people that we have a prescription for every problem in the world. If you can't get to sleep, we have a pill. If you can't stay awake, we

have a pill. If you want to gain weight, we have a pill. If you want

to lose weight we have a pill. If you're feeling depressed, we have a

pill, and since some of these pills cause you to feel suicidal, guess

what we have? We have a pill for you. If you want to stop

smoking... well you get the point. We are so into masking the

symptoms of a condition without curing the cause of it. Pills that

cause weight loss don't do anything for the lifestyle condition that

caused it. Anyone taking pills for depression can tell you that if

you stop taking the pills you go back to the depressed feelings.

You can't deal with an intangible situation with a tangible

treatment. My point is that we are sending a lot of mixed

messages to our youth and when they misinterpret our mixed

messages we get upset. And when we get upset we go to one of

our instant solutions. In this case our instant solution is to throw

them in jail. Throwing them in jail without helping them come up

with solutions to the situations that led them to commit the act

that caused their arrest is our version of a pill. When the

subscription (sentence) for the pill runs out, or the pill loses its effectiveness, guess what happens. They land right back in jail with a stronger prescription. This often means a longer sentence, but still with no real solution. This is something that I have firsthand experience with, since 100% of the guys I deal with come to my program from juvenile detention centers. These young men come into juvenile facilities with some serious issues, and instead of helping them deal with the issues, a lot of people choose to label them as losers, and criminals, and guess what most of them do when they get out. They return to the same environment without any new skills or tools to make a change. This is why I believe the client recidivism rate is so high. Now before I go any further, I want to take time to acknowledge the many workers in this field that really care, and devote their lives to making a difference. It is because of these wonderful people that we do see some measure of success, and change in the minds of these young men. These are the ones along with our clients that made working in these facilities a worthwhile and meaningful experience for me. Now since I have spoken about the people that make it a pleasure for me to work in such a great field, I can't help but feel compelled to talk about some of my pet peeves. In this field, the experts (front line workers) are forced to work under conditions that most licensing agencies, administrators, and even program managers (depending on whether or not they actually work directly with their staff and clients) don't have a clue about. They create rules, laws, and by-laws without ever rolling up their sleeves and experiencing what their workers must endure. Some even subscribe (pun intended) to an instant solution similar to some of the ones that I mentioned earlier. If the worker does not fully measure up to the company standards, instead of allowing their opinions to be heard, they are sometimes just fired. Who does this help? The company suffers, because they have missed out on an opportunity to gain firsthand knowledge from a true expert in the field that they specialize in, and now the worker, who has dedicated his/her time and energy to what the company stands for has to look for another job. Now there are exceptions of course because not all people that apply for these positions come in the field to really make a difference. Let's face it, some people are really just looking for a job, and while this job hunting quest could potentially develop into a true passion there is no real guarantee that it will. Come to think of it, there is no real guarantee that someone coming into the field with passion will even be able to endure the everyday challenges that almost always arise. That leads me to another point. Are there any real guarantees in life? Sure there are, but not too many in this field. Now that we have established this point, I would like to offer some strong advice to anyone willing to listen. Before you go out looking for any career, it would be very wise to do some soul searching to find what you really like. I can remember back in my senior year of high school thinking that a career in the army would be my best choice after graduation, since I really didn't know what I wanted to do with myself. In reality this went against just about everything I stood for since I didn't and still don't believe in killing, and don't see what moral purpose war serves. I wonder how my experience in an atmosphere filled with practices that I can't bring myself to agree with in the first place would have resulted in for me. The answer to that question is probably not too favorable. Now that I look back on that whole notion that I had of joining the army, I see that it was really a cop out on my part due to the fact that I hadn't done a self evaluation on my interests. Hey, if you feel that the army is the career for you, then go for it, but all I am saying that not everything is for everyone. I would also encourage parents to allow their children to decide what they feel is best for them, instead of pushing them into a career or decision that they most likely won't stick with anyway. So in that respect, sometimes it's a good thing when the apple falls far from the tree. But some people don't buy into the whole apple and tree concept at all. I would like to say that I don't even buy into it in the traditional sense. In actuality the apple and the tree could very well be the relationship between your thoughts and your actions, as what you do is usually dictated by what you think or believe.

Critical Thinking

What is your career goal?

Why did you pick this as a goal?

Would you perform the duties of this career for free?

Chapter 9

The Victim

Now that we have covered so much in the preceding chapters, let's review what we have learned. In chapter one I shared with you some of the most influential times in my life, and what led me to create this work. As you have learned, I was and still am very passionate about music, and encourage you to find your passion as early as possible in your life. I truly feel that when you find something that you truly love to do, and turn it into a career you will be much more likely to stick with it. In chapter two I spoke about my experiences working in a youth care facility for young men that had been arrested and referred to the program. I talked about how we are in a time now when giving stern lectures to children about what they need to be doing and what they are doing wrong just isn't as effective as it once seemed to be. As we moved into chapter three, the focus was on how we sometimes don't understand that it is okay to make mistakes as long as we can learn from them. It was also my intent to point out that there is rarely ever a time when quitting should be an obstacle unless you decide to quit a behavior that is truly holding you back. Then in chapter four I talked about the importance of positive associations. For example, you become more, and more like those that you choose to spend most of your time with. You would be hard pressed to find a monk in a singles bar wouldn't you. I can also make the point that you rarely find straight A students hanging out with truant students, or those that stay in detention. Chapter five, which is probably one of my favorites, focuses on people blaming others for their misfortunes. I talked about the guys blaming the police for arresting them after they have done something to be arrested for. This reminds me of a line that one of my Watusi group members, Mad Ak said regarding these situations. He questioned why "we touch poison ivy then complain about the irritation". That brings us to chapter six, where we learn the importance of living a life of non-judgment.

We have to realize that just as others shouldn't be able to dictate the way we live our lives, we must respect their wishes whether we like them or not. In chapter seven we learned that while we should be allowed to make our own decisions, there are time in our lives when we must learn to take heed to the advice of our loved ones for our own good. That brings us to chapter eight. This chapter tells us that the solution to everything we perceive as a problem lies within us. Now that we have had a brief summary of the previous chapters, let's move on. When I decided to write this book, I first decided to call it The Teenage Survival Handbook, but later felt that the title was lacking a specific identity. After spending weeks pondering this I decided to add the subtitle From Victim to Victor, but after more pondering, I decided to use From Victim to Victor as the main title, but kept Teenage Survival handbook for the subtitle. The word victim just kept standing out to me, so I decided to go deeper into the meaning of the word as my ongoing theme. So what exactly is a victim? According to the Webster's dictionary meaning, a victim is *a person who is deceived or cheated, as by his or her own emotions or ignorance, by the dishonesty of others.* When I read that definition I immediately realize that to avoid becoming a victim, you must first educate yourself about yourself. Eventually I settled on *Victory Is Yours!* as the title of the book. In most situations, ignorance is the main cause of poor decision making. If you are basing your decisions on what someone else wants you to do or on what someone else might think of you, you will likely be disappointed by the results your decisions yield. That is why I feel so strongly about the importance of finding your niche early in your life. The main benefit of doing this is that it creates a strong enough sense of self confidence that will allow you to resist other's negative influence on your choices. When you feel good about whom you are, you are less likely to make decisions that have undesirable effects on you. A person with a victim mind state doesn't value himself enough to want the best for his life. A victim is so focused on what the world owes him, and who's out to get him that he doesn't leave enough room in his life for success. This is a way of thinking that

plagues a lot of the guys I counsel in my program, and until they

learn to look at life differently, what we try to teach them will

never matter. How do you instill a sense of confidence in

someone that believes that no matter what they achieve in their

life, it will always be taken away from them? What do you say to a

person that comes from an environment that tells them that they

will never amount to anything? In the Webster's dictionary

definition it speaks about a victim being deceived or cheated by

the dishonesty of others. When you buy into the false information

of a system that tells you that you are destined for failure no

matter how hard you try, you put yourself in a situation that

makes life seem impossible to live. This is when you go into

survival mode. What should we expect them to think as a society

when we send them so many mixed signals? I recently saw a

commercial while watching television with my 9 year old son that

advertised a new toy gun. I know that on the surface this doesn't

seem serious, however, the gun advertised looked like a sniper's rifle or something that would be used in a war. It even had a laser scope on it to make sure you don't miss your target. I began to ask myself why someone would think of a tool that is used for killing as a toy. The question I probably should have been asking myself is why, we as parents don't find this to be an extreme contradiction of the moral we say we want our children to have. What happens when we turn on the news and witness a story about a school shooting? We are horrified, and wonder who introduced these children to these types of acts of violence? We tell the youth of today that we value education, but when we look at the reality of it, we can't help but notice the enormous amount of school closings that plague our cities. We tell them that getting a good job is very important, but how do we explain the unexplainable number of companies outsourcing their jobs to countries overseas. We talk about all the benefits of retiring from good jobs, but if we are honest with ourselves we must face the fact that our Social Security, Medicare, and pension systems are in deep trouble. We wonder where the sense of hope is on their parts, but we have not really given them a whole lot to feel hopeful about? With this being said, it is my opinion that even in the direst conditions, the most hopeless situations, our children are still willing to forgive us and accept our redirection. This inspires me to give another example (Get used to it folks, because this is what I do.). It seems that there was this wealthy older man, that we'll call Ted. Ted owned a very successful printing business that he was very proud of. He prided himself on the fact that he started with nothing and managed to become a self made millionaire. He owned an expensive Mercedes Benz that he was also very proud of. With every chance he got, he would look out of his office window and admire this thing of beauty, as he called it. At this point I would like to add that Ted was a bit conceited, and viewed most of his workers as being beneath him. He would always talk to them about the good old days when people "earned their keep". He would spend company meeting time lecturing about the value of a dollar, and always reminded his younger employees that they had it good. Ted had recently expanded his company by taking over another similar, but smaller company. To the surprise of many in the printing business, he decided to keep most of the workers from the smaller company. Ted needed to expand his building to accommodate the executives that he retained from the other company. This meant that he had to hire a construction company to add a new wing to the facility. Since Ted didn't trust the young crew (or any young people for that matter) that accepted the job, he decided to work evening shifts while they worked to make sure the job was done right. One day after putting in some late hours, Ted decided to take a break, and as usual went to the window to look at his beautiful Mercedes Benz. To his surprise, he saw a young man approaching his car. Immediately he panicked, and ran out of the building. As he ran towards the car he noticed that the young man had somehow managed to get the trunk opened, and looked to be going through his property. At this point Ted was in a rage, and approached the young man while shouting obscenities at him. The young man was speechless, as he was startled by Ted's erratic behavior.

"Didn't think I would catch you, did you, you little punk". The young man began to make an attempt answer him, but Ted immediately rushed him, wrestled him to the ground and demanded that he be silent. Out of desperation the young man attempted to speak once more, but this is when Ted completely lost it, and began to swing wildly at him. "You know it's punks like you that make the world the way it is", Ted shouted. "Someone call 911, while I teach this kid a lesson", shouted Ted. This went on for about ten more minutes until the police arrived. Before the officer could even get a word out, Ted began to bark out orders. "Take him away officer!" "I want to press full charges!" "He deserves whatever he gets"! "He probably has a record!" As the officer began to ask Ted for his information, Ted lost it again as he began to shout, "I know my rights junior!" "My taxes pay your salary; now get him out of here before I call your superiors!" The police officer calmly asked Ted for his registration, so he could proceed with the arrest. His response was "You're the one that's supposed to be doing that." "I'm not taking my eyes off this lowlife!" "You need to do that while I watch him." As the police entered the car, he had a confused look on his face, and asked Ted once again to show him his identification. "Well exactly who is the criminal here, him or me?" "Well actually, you are sir", responded the officer. "This car belongs to the gentleman you just assaulted." At this point, Ted was speechless, but finally mustered up enough energy to ask what was going on. "Well sir, the officer sarcastically responded", did you even take the time to ask this man what was going on before you decided to take matters into your own hands?" "What does that have to do with anything? ", screamed Ted. "What does it have to do with anything you ask?" the officer replied in a frustrated manner. "Sir, you have a beautiful car, but this isn't it", he said to Ted. "This car is registered to Jonathan Speilman. Is that you sir? Are you Jonathan Speilman? I am asking you this because if you are not Jonathan Speilman, I have no choice but to place you under arrest". Ted then thought out loud, "Well wait just a minute." "If this is not my car then just where is my car?"

replied Ted. At this point, Ted's victim struggled to stand up and said "your car is parked out front as usual sir. You have made a terrible mistake." Last week when you interviewed me and accepted my bid, I remarked about how we must have the same taste in vehicles. "I guess he was too busy ignoring you as he does everyone" responded one of the workers. Truly tragic isn't it. You see Ted was so full of himself that he automatically assumed the worst when he saw a young man approaching a nice vehicle. He didn't even realize that the car couldn't have been his as he was standing in the newly built area of his building that faces the back of his property. To Ted's surprise, his victim dropped all charges in court and still gave him a discount on the wonderful job he did. This probably sounds unrealistic to you, but if you think about how some parents abuse, and neglect their children, and the fact that these children still have unconditional love for them, the example I made earlier begins to seem very believable. It is this very reason why I say we have to take ownership for the conditions we put our youth in. When we refuse to acknowledge our part in today's conditions we are playing the victim. When we sit by and do nothing but complain about our failing school system, we are playing the victim. We as parents and responsible adults have to step up and take action. As Wayne Dyer would say, "Be the change that you wish to see". But there is another side of it. All of the ownership can't be placed on the parents, because at some point in your life you have to decide that you want better for yourself. When children refuse to honor their parents, they are playing the victim. When children believe the dreary images that are so popular in the media that talk about how all is lost, and that there is no hope, they are playing the victim. When a child purposely gets failing grades or acts out in school just to prevent his friends from realizing how smart he is to avoid being called a lame or nerd, he is indeed playing the victim. It is this very reason that causes some of the most intelligent young men and women to fall short of their goals in life. Remember that the reason most people fail is not because they set the bar too high and missed, but because they set the bar too low and hit. This is a very true statement that I hear in almost every motivational seminar I attend. If you don't want to appear smart, guess what will happen. What a lot of students don't realize or acknowledge is that this philosophy will come back to haunt you since most of the "friends" they want to impress don't have the power to hire them, or get them into college. It seems okay to "dumb yourself down" in school, but that is definitely not the image you want to have when you go into a job interview is it. Another way of playing the victim is when you complain. I can remember listening to Les brown as he told a story about dog that was heard moaning and moaning as he was lying down, and someone asked why he was moaning so loudly. The reason was that he was lying on a nail. The person asked why doesn't he just get up, and the reason was that the nail doesn't hurt enough. My point is that we often complain and complain about things without ever doing anything to change what we are complaining about. That's kind of like a football player sitting on the sideline complaining about how the coach doesn't know what he is doing because he hasn't put him I the game. Instead of complaining about the coach not putting him in the game, why doesn't he just go up to the coach and let him know that he is ready to play. How can you have an effect on the game when you just sit on the sidelines complaining? You shouldn't want to live your life as a backseat driver, or a Monday morning quarterback. Instead of playing the role of a victim, why don't you get up and do something about it?

Critical Thinking

Think of a situation in your life when you jumped to a conclusion.

Why do you think people are so quick to jump to conclusions?

Give a global example of jumping to a conclusion and how this

can be prevented.

Chapter 10

The victor

"I don't use my mind to think of myself as a victim or to complain about others". - Louise Hay

Okay, this is what it's all about isn't it. We all want to achieve a certain level of success in our lives, and would like to reach our goals. We want to feel as if our life has had some sort of meaning. I really love that quote by Louise Hay. To me, it really says that we are in full and complete control of our lives, and if we want to see positive changes, we must begin to look at things differently. We don't have to be a victim if we don't want to be. We have the power to achieve anything that we wish. Defining what we want out of life is the first step, but once we do that the question is how to obtain it. Before we get into how , I would first like to give examples of individuals that really inspired my life by overcoming circumstances that would cause most to view them as victims.

These wonderful human beings are not listed in any particular order. I love to read and listen to audio books recently came across to the work of Mr. Keith Harrell. I was recently listening to *Attitude plus Self-Confidence,* (which I highly recommend by the way) and was very moved as I listened to Keith speak about his childhood. Keith had an issue with stuttering, and told a very moving story about his first day in kindergarten. As Keith's the teacher asked for a volunteer to be the first student to introduce themselves to the rest of the class, she chose Keith and he began to stutter. Keith could have chosen to just give up after running home when his classmates began to laugh at him. What else would you expect a kindergartner to do, but this proved to be a mere stumbling block in his life, as he went on to become a world renowned speaker and author. In this respect Keith Harrell is truly a victor. I can remember back about 9 years ago as I was walking through a Media Play store as I waited for my wife (well actually we weren't married yet, but that's beside the point)as she was looking for a good book to read. I began to grow impatient as she took her time to find something that she could feel inspired by. I decide to kill some time by walking around the video section, and as I was on my way back to the book section, I passed the audio books and noticed a selection by Tony Robbins. He is one of my favorite speakers, but oddly enough, this story is not about him. After reading the back of his CD, I noticed that it was in the wrong section, and since I was trying to kill some time while my wife shopped, I began rearranging the CDs in alphabetical order. Then it happened. Out of the corner of my eye, I noticed a black and tan CD by the name of *Meditations for Manifesting* by Dr. Wayne W. Dyer. While I wasn't really into audio books, I felt compelled to purchase this one and was very impressed. My wife and I started listening to the CD every day, and I began searching for similar products. As of today I own over twenty Wayne Dyer books and CDs and have seen him live on many occasions. In many of his books, he openly discusses his past addictions, and how they became very impactful lessons for him, but the thing he cites as the most important lesson of his life is his father's decision to run out on the family during his early youth. This is an issue that plagues so many young men and women today, and one of the reasons a lot of them get to the point where they feel as if their life is over. I can speak from personal experience about the many levels of pain that are felt by a child when parents divorce, and wouldn't wish that feeling on anyone. In Dr. Dyer's case, not only did his dad walk out on his family, but he and his brother were placed in a foster home as his mom struggled to put the family back together. This is a seemingly insurmountable obstacle to most people, but Dr. Dyer has not only managed to come to terms with the pain he felt, but his outlook on how painful situations can actually be valuable lessons should be an inspiration to us all. It is this outlook that he has that shows that being a victim is not a part of his makeup. He is truly a victor. This is why many people call him the "father of motivation". I would like to say thank you Dr. Wayne Dyer for being an inspiration to me. In 1945, Les Brown was born in Liberty City in Miami, Florida. He is without a doubt one of the greatest motivational speakers of today. I think everyone would likely agree with me if they heard him speak, but what a lot of people don't know about him is that he and his twin brother Wes were born on the floor in an abandoned building. Now knowing this could have scared him for life, and caused him to view himself as worthless, but at six weeks old in stepped a wonderful woman by the name of Mamie Brown. She adopted Les and Wes and instilled in them a sense of self worth, and confidence that helped make him who he is today. In his life he has overcome many obstacles, from being labeled mentally retarded as a child in school, to his publicized divorce, and being diagnosed with cancer. Now any one of these setbacks would have stopped a lot of people dead in their tracks, but not Les Brown. Les has gone from being labeled slow in school to becoming a successful nightclub DJ, radio Dee Jay (look for *Step into Your Greatness* for this remarkable story), station manager, legislator, and world famous motivational speaker. Les brown through his actions has shown us what it means to overcome adversity, and is truly an inspiration to us all. There are so many others who have inspired me such as Keith Harrell, JB Glossinger, Iyanla Vanzant, and Bishop E Bernard Jordan, all of which have overcome adversity in their lifetimes. These people I have mentioned are true inspirations to me, but no one I know has set such an example of perseverance as Mary Phillips. Mary Phillips is my mother and a great source of inspiration to me as she has shown me first hand that no matter what you have been through in your life all is not lost until you decide that it is. My mother said something to me one time that I don't think she even knows changed my life. I remember driving one day in an area that I was not too familiar with and got turned around, so I decided to call my mom for directions as she was a school bus dispatcher at the time. She asked me where I was as I tried frantically to tell her my whereabouts. I was really frustrated to the point of almost panicking when she calmly said something that changed my life. She asked me if I had gas in the car, and I replied yes mama I have close to a full tank. She instantly responded by saying as long as you have gas in your tank, you are never lost. To you this might not sound like much, but it spoke volumes to me. At the time I was in between jobs and feeling a little lost in my life, but after I had time to actually ponder her words I decided to make some changes in my life. I translated her words to mean as long as you have energy and desire; there is nothing that can't be accomplished. Even when times are tough, and you are at your lowest point, a desire to make a change can work miracles. I tell this to the young men I counsel on a daily basis, because usually the thing holding them back is their belief that all is lost. I can recall very vividly that so many of the guys that have walked into my program came in hopeless, but when they were able to shift their energy to a more positive way of thinking everything changed for them. I can think of a lot of clients that have done a complete 180° change in results after first changing their thoughts about who they are and what they can accomplish. After having such a grim outlook on life and thinking that there was nothing out there for them, they finally realized that they were not lost because they still had gas in the tank. Have you ever watched professional teams that were known for their losing ways seemingly change their results overnight? I have seen this many times. I am reminded of the San Francisco Forty-Niners of the eighties. They went through a stretch of losing seasons and all of a sudden became five time Super Bowl winners. This happens in sports all the time and often because a team hired a new coach or drafted a key player or two. In their case they hired a new head coach who in turn drafted a brilliant quarterback. The coach and quarterback I'm speaking of are Bill Walsh and Joe Montana. So how do these teams make such a dramatic change? The changes I see are in the attitude these new players or coaches bring. I learned a little while ago that attitude equals energy. The most obvious difference between a victim and a victor is attitude. Teams like the Steelers, Forty-Niners, New England Patriots, Washington Redskins of the eighties, and nineties, Boston Celtics and Red Sox, Los Angeles Lakers, New York Yankees all have a winning attitude. They all expect to win. Losing for them is not an option, and if they do lose they view it as just a temporary setback. This is how you, the reader need to be. Losing is not an option. Choose what you want to do in your life and let nothing stop you from achieving your goal. If you don't reach your goal in your desired time, fill your tank up and go at it again, and again for as long as you need to. There will be times in your life when your goal will change and that is perfectly fine. My main point of advice is to choose something you love to do, because there is nothing worse than going into a career strictly for the money and hating going to work every day. I heard Les Brown speak about how the heart attack rate increases every Monday morning in America simply because a lot of people are going to jobs that they truly hate. Why would people want to do that to themselves? The most likely answer to that question is image. We sometimes paint this picture of ourselves as needing to portray a certain image to be considered successful. As Robert Kiyosaki points out in *Rich Dad Poor Dad*, most of us as children were told to do well in school, go to college get a degree and find a good company to work for. This way of thinking creates a lot of pressure for people and probably contributes to the increasing number of people on anti-depressants in this country. To be victorious in life it is my feeling that you must go with your heart as opposed to going with whatever image you think you need to be matched up with. Remember you are in control of your life and what you choose to do is nobody's business. When it's all said and done and you look back on your life I'm not too sure that what others thought about your decision on how you chose to live your life will really matter to you. What really matters in life is that you can comfortably look in the mirror in regards to your life and have a good feeling about the road you traveled. I've meet many people on many jobs in my work life that do nothing but complain about not following their dreams, and settling for what others somehow convinced them was the safest route to take. Remember that life is your movie so why allow another to step in a direct your script. This is a very delicate topic because even the most powerful and influential Hollywood directors and writers do often seek consultation from others. With that being said it would be beneficial to listen to those in your life that truly have your best interest at heart. To do this is definitely the way of the victor. I suggest you do your research on the topic to really see how important it is to not only pave your own way and follow your own script, but to seek the counsel from experts in your potential field.

Critical Thinking

Take time now to write a short summary of your life from the perspective of someone that doesn't know you personally but knows about you.

Chapter 11

Whose world is it?

"The world is actually in many key ways improving at the moment. There are still enormous challenges."- **Albert Einstein**

I can remember some years back listening to a song by Nas entitled *The World is Yours* in which he painted a visual verbal collage about getting the best of what life has to offer. Now I'll admit that the song might not be perceived by many as portraying a positive message, but one phrase in the first verse is very powerful to me. He said "the mind activation react like I'm facing time", and even though that precedes a reference to a controversial figure, those words as most of his words speak volumes. I interpret those words to mean that in our lives we often must react with urgency when we want to achieve our goals. We must realize that we and only we have the power to put our dreams into action. There will be many people in your life that will support your dreams and goals, but ultimately it is up to you to make those dreams and goals reality. I have been told countless times in my life that I could achieve this and I am capable of doing that, but many times I didn't feel a sense of urgency to act on these words of encouragement and therefore didn't make things happen. Are you able to be coached ("coachable")? This is what I hear a lot of prominent speakers say when they are speaking with the guys in my program. You can have all the talent in the world as I suspect just about every young man and women reading or listening to this has, but until you realize that you want to put your talents to use success will be extremely difficult. We must support our children in their endeavors, and to all the youth out there you must claim your power. This power that I speak of is like a small seed, freshly planted, and waiting harvest time. It is up to you to fertilize this seed of potential, by not only enjoying, but honoring you childhood. My advice to any young person reading this is to really get into this process of being a child. Do child things, act as a child, and above all else have fun. This is the one time in your life when you look back on it as an adult will seem to have flown by. This is also as I mentioned earlier the time when you are actually writing a script of what your adulthood will actually be like. This is your chance to create your "blueprint to success". I must also mention to parents that this is a time when we must allow our children to be children. Placing too much adult responsibility on our youth sometimes causes them to grow up too fast and miss critical rites of passage that can create a feeling of void in their adult lives. I've seen this first hand with family members and good friends that have had so many adult responsibilities as children for various reasons that caused them to go through stages of regression as adults. This is often the cause of grown men and women neglecting many of their parenting and professional duties, because they are attempting to recapture a part of their childhood that they feel they never had a chance to experience. Some adults have children but still think as a child, and this often causes the lines of parent and peer to become blurred. Just remember this children. You are in control of every decision you make, and it is completely up to you to accept the advice and guidance of the adults in your life. You make your own choices and must be prepared to live with the rewards and consequences of your decisions. This being said, I must stress to you the importance of making wise decisions. This means making your own decisions. I've spoken with many young guys that are in the situation they are in solely because they put too much faith in those that don't have their best interest at heart. The world of guns, drugs, gangs, unprotected sex (the cause of STDs, and unplanned pregnancies) and so many other pitfalls have to be introduced to people. It really breaks my heart when I speak to these young guys and realize the true potential they possess and how they have created so many obstacles that lessen their chance for success. I've heard it and said it many times; prisons and graveyards are full of geniuses. These young men that we as a society look at on the news and perceive to be the scum of the earth could have been surgeons, congressmen, motivational speakers, or perhaps the next candidates for President of the United States. Our children start out so innocent, and pure, but if they are not careful, and if we are not careful as parents, they can be tainted. Even as I am writing this, I am reminded about something my wife about how there is a certain part of the soul that remains receptive only to love and possibility. This untouchable inner child literally begs us to reconnect ourselves with it. This is probably why we hear so many stories about people that have led a life of crime that have somehow managed to turn things completely around. They have managed to reconnect with their true self, and let go of the world's corruption. So I would say to any teenager out there reading this, that you are not hopeless. You are not a lost cause. You can redeem yourself because no matter what you have been through, there is something inside of you that remembers your innocence. It is truly up to you and within your power to make things better for you and everyone around you. The world is depending on the success of the next wave of potential leaders. All it takes is a belief in yourself, and enough determination to walk the road of change. I am often amazed by ability of one person to impact the lives of those around them by deciding to change. Don't be afraid of what your boys might think if you change, because you could be the inspiration that they are praying for to give them a reason to change. This happens all the time. Change is made one person and one act at a time. Nothing in this world is impossible no matter how high the odds seem to be stacked against you. Take the 2008 presidential election for example. We have witnessed something that our ancestors would have never viewed as, or thought to be possible, and this is only the tip of the iceberg when it comes to your potential. What is your dream? Whatever it is, you are well within reach of attaining it if you only realize your power. The truth of the matter is that I am not telling you much of anything that you don't already know, and on a final note I would like to send you a message. Victory is indeed yours. You just have to accept it. You have to claim it. You have to make up your mind that nothing will stop you and your dream. After all that, there is only one question to ask. Are you willing to be victorious? If you answered yes to this question, with a little effort, and determination you will soon realize that, ***Victory Is Yours!***

Critical Thinking

If you were to put together a list of steps to improve your current situation with the most immediate actions needed being taken first, how would that list look?

Critical Thinking

What steps would you take to make your list a reality?

Critical Thinking

Remember to be very specific as this list will become your step by step blueprint to success.

Critical Thinking

What resources do you now have to assist you in completing the tasks on your list?

References:

Dyer, W. (2006) Inspiration, Your Ultimate Calling

Hicks, E & J (2004) Ask and It Is Given: The Law of Attraction

Harrell, K. (2004) Attitude Plus Self-Confidence: The Cornerstone of

Personal and Professional Success

Brown, L. (2004) Step Into Your Greatness

Glossinger, J.B. (2007) Get Out of Neutral

Tomer, S. (2007) YTB Red Carpet Days

Kiyosaki, R., Lechter, S. (2000) Rich Dad Poor Dad: What the Rich

Teach Their Kids About Money--That the Poor and Middle Class Do

Not!

For more information or to set up a phone or in person coaching session, please visit my website http://www.yestovictory.com

For more information on my new products, or to join my online support list, please leave your email address at foryourvictory@yahoo.com

Coming Soon from My wife Lakeetha Taylor; *Tea Medicine.* Check my website for updates on her project, and our other services.

www.ingramcontent.com/pod-product-compliance
Lightning Source LLC
LaVergne TN
LVHW091303080426
835510LV00007B/373